Reading

Comprehension

Louis Fidge

MACMILLAN FOUNDATION SKILLS

Macmillan Education
Between Towns Road, Oxford OX4 3PP
A division of Macmillan Publishers Limited
Companies and representatives throughout the world

ISBN 978-0-333-77683-4

Text © Louis Fidge 2001
Design and illustration © Macmillan Publishers Limited 2001

First published 2001

All rights reserved; no part of this publication may be reproduced, stored in a
retrieval system, transmitted in any form, or by any means, electronic,
mechanical, photocopying, recording, or otherwise, without the prior written
permission of the Publishers.

Illustrations by Debbie Clark/Beehive
Cover Illustration by Dave Mostyn
Cover Dsign by Linda Reed & Associates
Colour Separation by Tenon & Polert Colour Scanning Ltd

Printed and bound in Malaysia

2015 2014 2013 2012 2011
16 15 14 13 12

The authors and publishers wish to acknowledge, with thanks, the following
photographic sources:
Hutchison: p 58 (top) Christina Dodwell, pp 59 & 60 Robert Francis, p 58
(bottom) Edward Parker
Trip: p 12 E&J Bradbury

Acknowledgements

The author and publishers wish to acknowledge, with thanks, the following
who have kindly granted permission to use copyright material:

Lorna Evans: from *Martha's Mistakes* (Macmillan Education, 1991), by
permission of the publisher.
Terry Jennings: adapted from 'Fact File' in *Jungle Rescue* by Damian Morgan
(Macmillan Education, 1998), © Terry Jennings, by permission of Terry
Jennings and the publisher.
Moses Kainwo: 'I Visited a Village' from *On the Poetry Bus*, edited by David
Cobb (Macmillan Education, 1996), by permission of the author.
Janet Olearski: from *The Sunbird Mystery: 6A* (Macmillan English Language,
1998).
Daniel Postgate: adapted from *Kevin Saves the World* (David Bennett Books,
1994), © 1994 Daniel Bennett, by permission of the publisher. All rights
reserved.
Clive Sansom: 'The Airman' from *Speech Rhymes* (A & C Black, 1974), by
permission of the publisher.
Charles Thomson: 'My Pet Dinosaur' from *Dinosaur Poems*, edited by John
Foster (Oxford University Press, 1994), by permission of the author.

Every effort has been made to trace all copyright holders, but if any have been
inadvertently overlooked, the publishers will be pleased to make the necessary
arrangement at the first opportunity.

Contents

Skills, Scope and Sequence

Unit 1	**Maui makes the sun go slower**
Text Type	Myth (from New Zealand)
Text Level	Sentence completion
Sentence Level	Present and past tenses (irregular)
Word Level	Consonant digraph *qu*

Unit 2	**My pet dinosaur**
Text Type	Humorous poem
Text Level	Questions (literal/appreciative)
Sentence Level	Common nouns
Word Level	Consonant digraph *th*

Unit 3	**The old man and the strong man**
Text Type	Story with a moral issue
Text Level	Questions (literal/inferential)
Sentence Level	Categorising adjectives
Word Level	Similar sounds of *ow* and *ou*

Unit 4	**A newspaper report**
Text Type	Report
Text Level	True/false statements
Sentence Level	Speech marks (direct speech)
Word Level	Long and short *ea* sounds

Unit 5	**The airman**
Text Type	Shape poem
Text Level	Questions (appreciative/evaluative)
Sentence Level	Conjunctions
Word Level	Rhyming

Unit 6	**Kevin saves the world**
Text Type	Sci-fi/Fantasy adventure
Text Level	Correcting errors in statements
Sentence Level	Personal pronouns
Word Level	Use of apostrophes in contractions

Unit 7	**The magic dress**
Text Type	Fantasy
Text Level	Sequencing
Sentence Level	Personal pronouns
Word Level	Sound of *igh*

Unit 8	**Confucius – a very wise man**
Text Type	Autobiography
Text Level	Questions (literal/inferential/evaluative
Sentence Level	Pluralisation of nouns – change *f* to *v* and add *es*
Word Level	Similar sounds of *oi* and *oy*

Unit 9	**Different kinds of letters**
Text Type	Letter writing
Text Level	Features of presentation and layout/questions
Sentence Level	Focus on adverbs
Word Level	Changing adjectives into adverbs by suffixing with *ly*

Unit 10	**The danger of television!**
Text Type	Story with moral issue
Text Level	True/false statements
Sentence Level	Forming comparative and superlative adjectives
Word Level	Prefixing with *un* and *dis* – opposites

Unit 11	Hori, the greedy brother
Text Type	Story with a moral issue
Text Level	Sentence completion (multiple choice)
Sentence Level	Collective nouns
Word Level	Synonyms

Unit 12	Life in ancient Egypt
Text Type	Information text (non-chronological report)
Text Level	Features of the text/questions
Sentence Level	Simple present and past tense
Word Level	Changing nouns to adjectives by suffixing with *ful/less*

Unit 13	An alphabet of food
Text Type	Alphabetically-organised poem
Text Level	Features of poem/questions
Sentence Level	Adjectives (similes)
Word Level	Alphabetical order (first and second letters)

Unit 14	A good night's work
Text Type	Adventure story
Text Level	Questions (literal)
Sentence Level	Speech marks (direct speech)
Word Level	Letter patterns – *are, air, ear*

Unit 15	Famous explorers
Text Type	Information text
Text Level	Formatting information in form of chart
Sentence Level	Adverbs
Word Level	Syllabification

Unit 16	How to keep a bird diary
Text Type	Instructions
Text Level	Questions (literal/inferential/appreciative)
Sentence Level	Identifying grammatical errors in sentences
Word Level	Sound of *ir*

Unit 17	I visited a village
Text Type	Poem with patterned language and a moral
Text Level	Features of poem/questions
Sentence Level	Prepositions
Word Level	Soft *c* and *g* as in *ace* and *age*

Unit 18	Martha's mistakes
Text Type	Story with familiar setting
Text Level	Questions (literal/inferential/evaluative)
Sentence Level	General punctuation
Word Level	Sound of *ur*

Unit 19	Anansi and the alligator eggs
Text Type	Traditional story in form of a play
Text Level	Features of the play/questions
Sentence Level	Present, past and future tense
Word Level	Sounds of *er* and *or*

Unit 20	Endangered animals
Text Type	Information text (non-chronological report)
Text Level	Questions (literal/inferential/evaluative)
Sentence Level	Pluralisation of nouns – irregular nouns
Word Level	Prefixes – *en* and *re*

Teacher's Notes
Introduction to the series

The texts

Each book in the series introduces pupils to a wide range of culturally appropriate text types, including fiction, poetry and non-fiction. The books are carefully graded according to readability and are incremental in difficulty. The books provide a valuable complement to any other resources or series currently being used. The fact that each unit is structured in the same way makes the books accessible and easy to use.

The related activities

The related activities support the development of essential reading skills at *Text Level*, encouraging pupils to read at different levels including literal, inferential and evaluative comprehension skills. The stimulus passages are also used to help pupils develop skills at *Sentence Level* (grammar and punctuation) and *Word Level* (spelling and vocabulary).

The Skills, Scope and Sequence Chart

The *'Skills, Scope and Sequence Chart'* (on pages 2 – 3) provides an immediate overview of text types included and skills being developed at *Text, Sentence* and *Word Level*. This chart is very helpful for planning purposes.

Using the books

To gain maximum benefit from the books, it is suggested that they are used systematically, working through each unit one at a time, in the given order. However, the books may also be used flexibly, selecting units as desired to complement other work being done in class.

Tackling the texts

The stimulus texts may be tackled in a variety of ways. They could be used for shared reading. This could take the form of the teacher reading the whole text to the class or inviting different pupils to contribute as appropriate. Certain texts e.g. poems, provide an ideal opportunity for whole class participation. Alternatively, the pupils could be asked to read the text silently or read it aloud in pairs or in groups. Whatever approach is used, to make the most of each text it should be discussed to ensure pupils have a good grasp of the literal meaning of the text and any vocabulary they may not have met before. The related *Text Level* activities may initially be done as a class verbally to help pupils reflect on the texts.

Tackling the related activities

The related activities at *Text, Sentence* and *Word Level* may be used systematically or selectively as desired. However they are used, it is suggested that prior to working any activity there is some discussion with the pupils to ensure they understand what is required of them.

Teaching Features
Units of work

There are 20 units of work (of either two, three or four pages in length). Each unit is structured in the same way i.e. a stimulus text, followed by three different levels of activities (*Text*, *Sentence* and *Word Level*).

Unit number and title

Text Level activities (a range of differentiated comprehension tasks)

Sentence Level activities (Grammar or punctuation tasks)

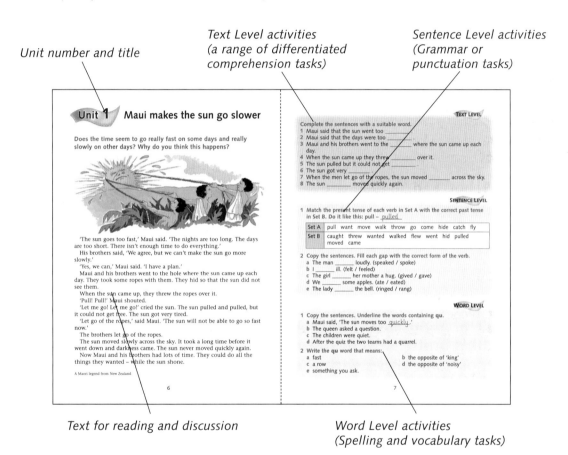

Text for reading and discussion

Word Level activities (Spelling and vocabulary tasks)

The Glossary (pages 62–64)

This explains and gives examples of key language terms and concepts covered in the activities. The glossary may be used for teaching purposes or for reference by pupils.

Unit **1** Maui makes the sun go slower

Does the time seem to go really fast on some days and really slowly on other days? Why do you think this happens?

'The sun goes too fast,' Maui said. 'The nights are too long. The days are too short. There isn't enough time to do everything.'

His brothers said, 'We agree, but we can't make the sun go more slowly.'

'Yes, we can,' Maui said. 'I have a plan.'

Maui and his brothers went to the hole where the sun came up each day. They took some ropes with them. They hid so that the sun did not see them.

When the sun came up, they threw the ropes over it.

'Pull! Pull!' Maui shouted.

'Let me go! Let me go!' cried the sun. The sun pulled and pulled, but it could not get free. The sun got very tired.

'Let go of the ropes,' said Maui. 'The sun will not be able to go so fast now.'

The brothers let go of the ropes.

The sun moved slowly across the sky. It took a long time before it went down and darkness came. The sun never moved quickly again.

Now Maui and his brothers had lots of time. They could do all the things they wanted – while the sun shone.

A Maori legend from New Zealand

Complete the sentences with a suitable word.
1 Maui said that the sun went too ___slow__.'
2 Maui said that the days were too ___big___.
3 Maui and his brothers went to the ___East__ where the sun came up each
   day.
4 When the sun came up they threw ___ropes__ over it.
5 The sun pulled but it could not get ___free__ .
6 The sun got very ___tired__ .
7 When the men let go of the ropes, the sun moved ___slowly__ across the sky.
8 The sun ___had__ moved quickly again.

1 Match the present tense of each verb in Set A with the correct past tense
   in Set B. Do it like this: pull – _pulled_

Set A	pull want move walk throw go come hide catch fly
Set B	caught threw wanted walked flew went hid pulled moved came

2 Copy the sentences. Fill each gap with the correct form of the verb.
   a The man __spoke__ loudly. (speaked / spoke)
   b I __felt__ ill. (felt / feeled)
   c The girl __gave__ her mother a hug. (gived / gave)
   d We __ate__ some apples. (ate / eated)
   e The lady __rang__ the bell. (ringed / rang)

1 Copy the sentences. Underline the words containing **qu**.
   a Maui said, 'The sun moves too _quickly_ .'
   b The queen asked a question.
   c The children were quiet.
   d After the quiz the two teams had a quarrel.

2 Write the **qu** word that means:
   a fast __quickly__   b the opposite of 'king' __queen__
   c a row __quarrel__   d the opposite of 'noisy' __quiet__
   e something you ask. __question__

Unit 2 My pet dinosaur

Do you have a pet? What is it? Does it ever cause any problems?

My dinosaur
Was getting thinner
And so I brought him
Home for dinner.

He ate as fast
As he was able;
He ate the food,
He ate the table.

He ate the fridge,
He ate the chair,
He ate my favourite
Teddy bear.

He is a very
Naughty pet.
He even ate
The TV set.

Charles Thomson,
from *Dinosaur Poems*
(Oxford University Press)

1 What is the poem about? *A dinosaur eating things*
2 What is the poet's name? *Charles thompson*
3 Why did the poet bring the dinosaur home? *because he was getting thin*
4 Name six things the dinosaur ate. *table, teddy bear, food, tv set, fridge,*
5 Why does the poet call the dinosaur 'naughty'? *because he at every thing*
6 How many verses are there in the poem? *16*
7 Write a word in the poem that rhymes with:
   a thinner   **b** able   **c** chair   **d** pet *a.dinner b.table c.bear d.set*
8 Write something you liked (or disliked) about the poem.
I really liked Rhyming coplets.

SENTENCE LEVEL

1 **Copy the sentences. Think of a suitable noun for each gap.**
   a A *builder* builds houses.
   b A *teacher* teaches children.
   c A *doctor* makes people better.
   d A *dentist* looks after our teeth.

2 **Match each noun with its definition.**
   a A bridge   is a place for keeping a car.
   b A garage   is a place where crops are grown.
   c A shop   is a place where people cross a river.
   d A farm   is a place where you can buy things.

3 **Make up your own definition for each of these things:**
   a fridge   **b** table   **c** chair   **d** a television set

WORD LEVEL

1 **Write these th words in two sets:**
   a words beginning with **th**   **b** words ending with **th**

   | thin | cloth | thing | tooth | path | thick | thank | bath | think | both |

2 **Write the th word that means:**
   a not thick   *thin*   **b** what you do with your brain   *think*
   c something you walk on   *path*   **d** something you put water in   *bath*
   e something in your mouth   *tooth*   **f** two   *both*

3 **Add th and write the new words you make.**
   a *th* is   **b** *th*at   **c** *th*en   **d** *th*an   **e** *th*cy   *throw*

Unit 3 The old man and the strong man

'It is better to be wise than strong.' Do you agree?

Long ago there was a town with a busy marketplace. People came to buy and sell all sorts of things there.

One day an old man went to the market to buy some vegetables. He saw lots of people. In the middle of them was a strong man. Everyone was afraid of him.

The strong man had a big heavy rock with him. Some people tried to lift it but it was too heavy for them.

The strong man said, 'Look at me. I can lift this heavy rock.'

The man bent down and took hold of the heavy rock. He pulled and pulled. His face went redder and redder. Slowly he lifted the rock above his head.

'I am the strongest man in the world,' he cried.

Then someone shouted, 'You are just like a buffalo! A buffalo is strong too, but it has no sense!' The people all laughed.

The strong man was angry. He saw the old man smiling.

'Why are you smiling?' he shouted at him.

The old man said, 'You may be strong, but you are very proud. You cannot laugh at yourself.'

The strong man felt foolish. He looked down at the ground and walked away. After that, no-one was afraid of him any more.

1 Where did the story take place? *in busy marketplace*
2 What did the old man want to buy in the market? *Vegetables*
3 Who was in the middle of all the people? *a strong man*
4 Why do you think everyone was afraid of the strong man? *he though kill k*
5 What happened as the strong man lifted the heavy rock? *his face wentred*
6 Why did everyone laugh at the strong man? *because he was angry*
7 How do you know the strong man was angry with the old man? *fool,sh*
8 What did the old man say that made the strong man feel foolish? *bufallo*

Draw a chart and sort the adjectives into three sets.

big	rough	soft	prickly	small	sweet
hard	bitter	tall	smooth	large	hairy
sour	wide	salty	long	huge	savoury

adjectives to do with texture (the feel of things)	adjectives to do with taste	adjectives to do with size
rough *hard big sour*	sweet *Prickly small large*	big *huge big large*

1 Copy these words. Underline the **ow** or **ou** in each word.

| t<u>ow</u>n sh<u>ou</u>t c<u>ow</u> c<u>ou</u>nt f<u>ou</u>nd m<u>ou</u>th <u>ow</u>l cr<u>ow</u>n cl<u>ou</u>d fl<u>ow</u>er |

2 Copy this sentence. Think of a suitable word to complete it.
   In some words **ow** and **ou** sound the *ow* .

3 Copy the sentences. Use some of the **ow** and **ou** words to complete them.
   a We get milk from a *cow* .
   b I can *count* to a hundred.
   c There was a big black *cloud* in the sky.
   d The king wears a *crown* on his head.
   e I lost my pen and then *found* it again.
   f I picked a *flower* from the garden.

11

Unit 4   A newspaper report

How important are headlines in newspapers? What do you think this newspaper report is about?

STORMS STRIKE STEVENAGE

Mr Smith's home with its roof missing

Last night **severe** storms struck the town of Stevenage. They caused lots of **damage** to homes and other buildings. One man was going to bed when the wind blew the roof off his house. 'I was just getting into bed. The wind was very strong. There was a terrible noise. When I looked up I could see the moon and the stars! My roof was missing!' Mr Smith said.

The storm caused lots of problems on the roads as well. A bus blew off a bridge. Jenny Tan, the bus driver, said, 'A strong wind **spun** my bus round when it was on the bridge. Luckily there was no-one in the bus. I opened the door and jumped to safety. I saw my bus crash and fall into the river below. It was very frightening.'

One lorry driver had a lucky escape when a tree blew over onto his lorry. Mr Bob Bell said, 'Suddenly the wind **uprooted** a huge tree. It crashed down onto the back of my lorry. It nearly hit my head. I am lucky to be alive.'

People who were injured during the storm were taken to the local hospital. The doctors have been very busy. Dr Lee commented, 'It was a terrible night. There were many accidents for us to deal with. We worked all through the night. I don't want another night like that!'

Read the report and say if each sentence is true or false.
1 Storms struck the town of Stevenage. T
2 The wind blew the door off Mr Smith's house. F
3 A car blew off a bridge. F
4 Jenny Tan is a bus driver. T
5 Jenny Tan jumped to safety before the bus fell into the river. T
6 A bridge blew over onto a lorry. F
7 Injured people were taken to a hospital a long way away. T
8 The doctors at the local hospital were very busy all night. T

Copy the sentences. Put in the missing speech marks.
1 Mr Smith said, The wind was very strong.
   Mr Smith said, 'The wind was very strong.'
2 Jenny Tan said, I drive a bus.
3 Mr Bell said, I had a crash in my lorry.
4 Dr Lee said, You have broken your leg.
5 Mrs Jones said, I am going to the shop.
6 May I have a cup of tea? Gemma asked.
7 Keep quiet! the teacher shouted.
8 It's a lovely day, Tom said.

1 Copy these words. Complete them with ea.

a n ea r   b h ea d   c ea gle   d br ea d   e n ea tly
f l ea p   g spr ea d   h b ea n   i f ea ther   j b ea k
k r ea dy   l thr ea d   m cl ea n   n w ea ther   o sp ea k

2 Copy this chart. Use the words in 1 above to fill it in.

words in which **ea** sounds like **ee** as in b**ee**	words in which **ea** sounds like **e** as in r**ed**
near bean clean speak	head said thread ready

13

Unit 5 — The airman

What do you notice about the way this poem is set out?

rrrrrrrrrr
The engine roars,
The propeller spins,
'Close the doors!'
Our flight begins.

zzzzzzzzzz
The plane rises;
It skims the trees.
Over the houses
We fly at our ease.

mmmmmmmmmm
ZOOM goes the plane,
The engine hums.
Then home again,
And down it comes...
       mmmm
         m
           m
         m
      mmmm
   z
 z
  z
   zzzzrrrrrrrrrr

Clive Sansom, from
Speech Rhymes (A & C Black)

1 What word in the first verse tells you that the engine makes a loud noise? *roars*
2 What word in the first verse tells you how the propeller moves? *spins*
3 Who do you think says 'Close the doors.'? *pilot*
4 What word in the second verse means 'goes up'? *rises*
5 What word in the second verse tells you that the plane passes near the trees? *skims*
6 What word in the third verse tells you that the plane is going fast? *zoom*
7 What word in the third verse tells you that the engine is making a quieter noise? *hum*
8 How the pictures help you understand what the poem is about?

Copy these pairs of sentences. Choose the conjunction **because**, **if** or **when** to join them.
1 The pilot started the engine. It was time to go.
   The pilot started the engine because it was time to go.
2 I hurt my ankle. I played football yesterday.
3 The monkey will get some bananas. It climbs the tree.
4 I had a drink. I was thirsty.
5 We will get wet. It rains.
6 I will buy some sweets. I get some money.
7 Peter was late for school. He overslept.
8 The boy will break the window. He throws a stone.

1 Find and write the ten pairs of rhyming words in the word wall.

spin	house	match	loud	wise
marry	proud	tree	bread	sky
down	head	bee	catch	carry
mouse	begin	fly	rise	frown

2 Think of one more rhyming word to go with each pair in 1 above.
   Sea Ice

Unit 6 Kevin saves the world

What sort of things are you really good at?

Kevin wasn't very good at anything. He wasn't very good at getting to school on time. He wasn't very good at painting, or sport, or spelling. But he was good at one thing – making silly faces.

One day a spaceship landed in Kevin's back garden. Out of it climbed a monster. 'I have come from a far-off planet,' said the monster.

'Come in,' said Kevin. 'I'll make you something to eat.'

But cooking was another thing Kevin wasn't very good at. He mixed cornflakes with **baked beans**, chocolate sauce with tinned fish, and jam with **curry** powder, then mopped up the mess with a dish cloth.

The monster took a huge mouthful.

'Yeeeuchh!' it yelled. 'This is **revolting**! Give me a drink to take the taste away!'

Kevin poured some orange juice into a glass, then slipped and spilt it down the monster's **front**.

'Horrid!' cried the monster. 'Nasty, sticky, orange juice all down my front! Isn't there anything you're good at?'

'Yes!' said Kevin and made a face.

'AAAAAARGH!' cried the horrified monster. He ran out to his spaceship, got in and flew off.

'Kevin! What have you been doing?' cried his mother when she saw the mess in the kitchen.

'I've been saving the world, Mum!' said Kevin.

Adapted from story by Daniel Postgate (David Bennett Books Ltd.)

16

One word in each sentence is wrong. Write each sentence correctly.
1 Kevin wasn't very good at <u>printing</u>, or sport, or spelling.
2 Kevin was good at making silly <u>races.</u>
3 One day a <u>helicopter</u> landed in Kevin's garden.
4 A <u>man</u> climbed out of the spaceship.
5 Kevin made the monster some food to <u>wear</u>.
6 Kevin spilled some <u>apple</u> juice over the monster.
7 When Kevin made a face, the monster <u>walked</u> out to his spaceship.
8 Kevin said, 'I've been <u>seeing</u> the world, Mum!'

Choose the best pronoun to fill each gap.
1 Kevin was not good at spelling but <u>he</u> was good at making faces. (he / she)
2 The lady was old. _____ was tired. (He / She)
3 _____ am tall for my age. (I / We)
4 The children laughed as _____ ran along. (it / they)
5 'Where are _____ going?' the teacher asked. (you / he)
6 _____ like singing. (It / We)
7 The dog stopped and _____ barked loudly. (you / it)
8 _____ is raining. (You / It)

1 Copy the lists. Match up each contraction with its longer form.

Contractions	Longer forms
isn't	does not
wasn't	you are
doesn't	is not
she's	we will
it's	was not
you're	it is
I've	I am
we'll	she is
I'm	I have

2 Make up some sentences of your own. Use each of the contractions above.

Unit 7 The magic dress

Do you wish you could fly? What would it be like? Where would you go?

One day Becky went shopping. She stopped to look at some dresses. Becky saw a lovely dress with different coloured stripes, like a rainbow. It was just what she wanted. Becky had enough money so she decided to buy it. When she touched the dress, Becky felt a strange feeling of excitement, as if there was something very special about it.

Becky hurried home and tried the dress on. As she did so, she felt very **odd**. She started to float in the air and fly like a bird! The dress was magic!

She flew up and up and up, high in the sky. She flew high above the clouds. When she looked down, everything looked smaller – the cars looked like **beetles** and the people looked as small as ants! Her house looked like a little box!

Becky flew over the sea. She waved to the people on boats below.

They were very surprised! She waved to the whales. They blew water into the air at her. She waved to the dolphins. They jumped out of the water when they saw her.

Becky flew over the jungle. She waved to the tigers. They growled at her. She waved to the elephants. They lifted their trunks and **trumpeted** at her. She waved to the monkeys. They threw bananas at her.

Becky flew over the desert. It was very hot. She waved to the camels. She waved to the snakes. She waved to people in tents in the **oasis**.

Becky flew over the snow and ice. The bears and penguins were pleased to see her, but it was very cold.

Becky began to get tired so she flew home and landed in her garden. What an adventure! What a dress!

19

Rewrite these sentences, in order, so that they tell the story.
- Becky flew over the sea and saw some whales.
- When she tried the dress on, Becky started to float in the air.
- In the desert Becky saw some camels.
- Becky bought a new dress.
- When Becky flew over the jungle, some monkeys threw bananas at her.
- Last of all, Becky flew over the snow and ice.
- When she flew over her house, it looked like a little box.

SENTENCE LEVEL

Who or what does each underlined pronoun stand for?
1 Becky bought a dress and tried <u>it</u> on. _the dress_
2 Becky has a cat. <u>She</u> likes the cat a lot.
3 '<u>We</u> like sweets,' Ben and Becky said.
4 Becky saw a whale. <u>It</u> was enormous.
5 The man wanted the car but it was too expensive for <u>him</u>.
6 'Can <u>you</u> come and play?' Ali asked Shireen.
7 'Make <u>me</u> a cup of tea, please,' Mrs Cork asked Jason.
8 Tom ran for the bus but <u>he</u> missed it.

WORD LEVEL

1 Make some new words. Change the **s** in **sight** to:
  a l<u>ight</u>   b m_____
  c t_____   d r_____
  e f_____   f n_____
  g fr_____   h sl_____
  i br_____   j fl_____

2 Choose the correct word to complete each sentence.
  a I turned on the _____ in my bedroom. (bright / light)
  b My shorts are too _____ . (tight / might)
  c The mountains were a lovely _____ . (fight / sight)
  d The monster gave me a _____ . (flight / fright)
  e I woke up in the middle of the _____ . (right / night)

20

Unit 8 — Confucius – a very wise man

Do we only learn things at school? How else can we learn about the world?

Over 2,000 years ago, in China, there lived a boy called Confucius. When he was only three, his father died. His mother was very poor. In those days people had to pay to go to school and his mother did not have enough money to send him.

As Confucius grew up he wanted to learn things. So he decided to teach himself. Unfortunately he was a strange-looking boy. The other children pointed and made fun of him. They called him names and laughed at him. Confucius got very upset, but he was a kind, gentle boy and did not fight back.

Confucius did not play with other children. He went off to talk to holy men in the temple and learnt from them. He talked to artists and musicians and learnt from them. If he tried to do something difficult, he kept trying over and over again until he learnt how to do it. In this way the boy taught himself to read and write and learnt lots of interesting things. Confucius grew up to be a very clever man.

When he was a man, Confucius became the **mayor** of the city of Changtu. People were very happy when he was their leader because he was a wise ruler. He used his abilities and **skills** in a **sensible** and fair way.

People sometimes call him the wisest man who ever lived. We still remember many of his wise sayings today.

21

Here are some of the sayings of Confucius.

Use your eyes and you will see many wonderful things.

Use your ears to listen and learn.

Always make sure that you have a friendly smile which tells other people you are kind.

Always remember to be well-mannered and polite.

Always speak the truth.

Always **play fair** with others.

Do not do anything to other people that you would not like someone to do to you.

1 How long ago did Confucius live? *8 centrys ago*
2 Where was he born? *Mangolian land*
3 What sentence tells you that Confucius did not go to school?
4 a Why did other children laugh at Confucius?
   b Do you think this was kind?
5 What sort of people did Confucius learn from?
6 What did Confucius do if he found something difficult?
7 In which ways was Confucius a wise ruler?
8 Which of the sayings of Confucius do you think is most important? Say why.

SENTENCE LEVEL

1 **Write the plural of each noun.**
   a one life but two _lives_
   b one knife but two _____
   c one wolf but two _____
   d one loaf but two _____
   e one shelf but two _____
   f one thief but two _____

2 **Write the singular of each noun.**
   a one _leaf_ but two leaves
   b one _____ but two halves
   c one _____ but two calves
   d one _____ but two wives

3 **Copy and complete this rule:**
In many nouns ending with **f** or **fe** we change the __ to __ and add __ to make the nouns plural.

WORD LEVEL

1 **Copy these words. Underline the oi or oy in each word.**

b<u>oy</u> p<u>oi</u>nt joy coin voice toy annoy noise destroy join

2 **Copy these sentences. Think of a suitable word to complete each sentence.**
   a In some words **oi** and **oy** sound the _____ .
   b The letters **oy** usually come at the _____ of a word.
   c The letters **oi** usually come in the _____ of a word.

3 **Which oi or oy word means:**
   a the opposite of a girl
   b something you play with
   c money
   d to upset
   e happiness
   f to fix two things together

Unit 9 Different kinds of letters

Why do people write letters? Here are three very different letters to read.

An invitation

Hazyview
PO Box 134
Vancouver
British Columbia
Canada

10 January 2001

Dear Susan

It seems a long time since we last saw you. Uncle John and I would love you to come and stay with us for a short holiday. We can do some shopping and go on some visits. You can help on the farm some days. I have spoken to your mother and she says it is fine. I enclose a train ticket and will meet you at the station.

Love

Aunt Grace

A letter to parents

Hazyview
PO Box 134
Vancouver
British Columbia
Canada

10 February 2001

Dear Mum and Dad
I am having a lovely time at Auntie Grace's. It is lovely on the farm. Every day
I help Uncle John and Aunt Grace with the jobs. They are very kind to me. We
have been for a walk in the mountains. I saw an enormous waterfall. Aunt Grace
took me into the city. It was very busy. There were so many people and so much
traffic. We went shopping and Aunt Grace bought me a new dress. It is lovely. It
is red with yellow spots on it. The time is passing very quickly. I enclose a photo of
me in my new dress.
I miss you all but I am enjoying myself.

Lots of love
Susan

A letter of thanks

PO Box 24
High Prairie
Alberta
Canada

5 March 2001

Dear Aunt Grace and Uncle John
I am just writing to tell you that I arrived home safely. I got very tired on the
train and nearly fell asleep and missed my station!
Thank you so much for inviting me to come and stay. I loved helping on the farm.
Perhaps I will work on one when I get older. You were very kind to me while I was
there. I enjoyed every minute, especially the trip to the mountains. The huge
waterfall was the most wonderful I have ever seen in my life. Mum thinks the
dress you bought me is really nice. She wishes that she had one too!
I will never forget my lovely holiday with you.
Mum and Dad send their best wishes.

Lots of love
Susan

1 What does each letter have in the top right-hand corner?
2 Who is each person writing to?
3 Who wrote:
   a the invitation?   b the letter to parents?   c the thank-you letter?
4 a Why did Aunt Grace write to Susan?
   b What did she enclose in her letter?
5 What did Susan do at Aunt Grace's?
6 Why did Susan write to Aunt Grace when she returned from her holiday?
7 In her letter to Aunt Grace, how does Susan say she nearly missed her station?
8 Draw a rectangle the size of an envelope. In it, write either your name and full address or the name and address of your school.

SENTENCE LEVEL

1 **Copy the sentences. Underline the adverb in each sentence.**
   a Susan spelt the word <u>correctly</u> .   b The lion roared loudly.
   c The little girl smiled sweetly.   d We did the sums easily.
   e The boy ran quickly.   f I crossed the road carefully.

2 **Think of a suitable adverb to go in each gap.**
   a The two children argued _____ .   b I whispered _____ .
   c Mrs Khan laughed _____ .   d Susan ate _____ .
   e The man slept _____ .   f I painted the picture _____ .

WORD LEVEL

1 **Make adverbs from these adjectives.**
   a clever – <u>cleverly</u>   b sudden – _____
   c quiet – _____   d fair – _____
   e careful – _____   f safe – _____
   g brave – _____   h kind – _____
   i bad – _____   j equal – _____

2 **Make adverbs from these adjectives.**
   a noisy – <u>noisily</u>   b angry   c easy   d hungry   e lazy

3 Write a rule for changing **busy** to **busily**. Explain what you have to do.

4 Write the adjectives which come from these adverbs.
   a gently – <u>gentle</u>   b simply   c horribly   d sensibly   e miserable

Unit 10 The danger of television!

What are the good things about television? What are the bad things?

Mr Chips was a lovely old man. He always had a smile on his face. Mr Chips loved people. He always had a kind word to say to everyone. Mr Chips loved his garden, where he grew flowers and vegetables. Everyone liked Mr Chips.

Everything was fine – until the day he got a television **set**. Mr Chips decided to buy a television set because he was lonely in the evenings when he had nothing to do.

Mr Chips thought television was wonderful. He loved to watch sport. He loved to watch films. But best of all he loved to watch the advertisements. Mr Chips thought they were as good as all the shows.

But soon Mr Chips began to get annoyed. He was only able to watch one channel at a time. He was missing all the other good programmes on the other channels. He decided to buy a video to record the programmes he was missing. Everything was fine for a short time.

27

Then Mr Chips got annoyed again. When he went into the kitchen to make himself something to eat he was not able to watch television. So he moved his kitchen into his living room! He moved in his cooker and his fridge. He moved his bed in as well. He did not have to leave his room at all. He spent all day and most of the night watching television.

He did not have time to do any more gardening so he sold his garden. He spent the money he got on more television sets. Now he had lots of television sets in his room. He had a different programme on each set. He watched lots of programmes at the same time. It was very noisy.

Soon there was no room for any more television sets. His room was full of them but Mr Chips did not care. He did not go out anymore. He never saw his friends. He never talked to anyone. The only thing he ever did was watch television. Mr Chips had become a television addict!

Read the story and say if each sentence is true or false.
1 At first Mr Chips loved his garden.
2 Mr Chips decided to buy a television set because he wanted to watch sport.
3 Mr Chips thought the advertisements were as good as the shows.
4 Mr Chips got a video so he could record the programmes he was missing.
5 Mr Chips moved his television set into the bathroom.
6 Mr Chips spent every minute of every day watching television.
7 Mr Chips sold his garden because he did not have any time to do any gardening.
8 In the end Mr Chips became a television addict.

1 **Write the comparative and superlative form of each adjective.**
   a new – _newer – newest_   b slow   c hard   d small   e wild
2 **Write the comparative and superlative form of each adjective.**
   a large – _larger – largest_   b pale   c strange   d brave   e white
3 **Write the comparative and superlative form of each adjective.**
   a hot – _hotter – hottest_   b big   c thin   d wet   e fat
4 **Write the comparative and superlative form of each adjective.**
   a happy – _happier – happiest_   b lonely   c lucky
   d dry   e noisy

1 **Add the prefixes. Make the words.**

a

un	happy
	pack
	well
	fair

b

dis	agree
	obey
	trust
	cover

2 **Copy the sentences. Change the underlined word so that it means the opposite, by adding either the prefix un or dis. The first is done for you.**
a Mr Chips was very <u>happy</u>.
   <u>Mr Chips was very unhappy.</u>
b I <u>agreed</u> with everything the man said.
c I felt quite <u>well</u>.
d When we get home we <u>pack</u> our bags.
e The children always <u>obey</u> me.

Unit 11 Hori, the greedy brother

What makes a person greedy? What are greedy people like?

Hori and Mosi were very sad when their parents died. Hori was the oldest. He took care of things.

'Our parents did not leave us much,' Hori said to Mosi. 'They left the house to me. I will live in it. They left you the piece of land near the mountain, and the cat and dog.'

Hori was greedy. He did not tell Mosi that their parents also left both of them a lot of money. He kept it all for himself.

Mosi went to **plough** the land near the mountain. It was hard work, because he only had the cat and dog to pull **the plough**. When the Master of the Mountain saw this, he opened his mouth wide and roared with laughter. As he laughed, the mountain split open. Inside, Mosi saw a pile of gold. Quickly, he filled a sack with gold and ran out. The Master of the Mountain stopped laughing and the mountain closed again.

Mosi went to tell his brother Hori about his good luck. Hori wanted some gold, too. He asked Mosi to lend him the cat and dog.

The next day, Hori went to plough the land near the mountain, with the cat and dog. When the Master of the Mountain saw this, he opened his mouth wide and roared with laughter. As he laughed, the mountain split open. Hori ran inside and greedily, began to fill up lots of sacks with gold. Just then the Master of the Mountain saw Hori. Angrily, the Master of the Mountain shut his mouth and trapped Hori inside the mountain.

Hori was never seen again. Mosi got the house, all the land and all the money which was really his.

Choose the best word to fill each gap.
1 Hori and Mori were _____ when their parents died.
  (afraid / happy / sad)
2 Hori was the _____ brother. (biggest / fattest / oldest)
3 Hori was _____ . (poor / greedy / nice)
4 Mori only had the cat and dog to pull the _____. (cart / sack / plough)
5 Mori found a pile of _____ inside the mountain. (jewels / mud / gold)
6 Mori told Hori about his good _____ . (luck / friend / wife)
7 Hori was _____ inside the mountain. (lost / trapped / locked)
8 Hori was _____ seen again. (often / always / never)

Choose the correct collective noun to fill each gap.
1 a _pile_____ of gold (pile / bunch)
2 a _____ of grapes (bunch / bundle)
3 a _____ of books (flock / library)
4 a _____ of sheep (chest / flock)
5 a _____ of matches (pile / box)
6 a _____ of drawers (box / chest)
7 a _____ of cows (herd / shoal)
8 a _____ of bees (swarm / flock)

1 Copy the words. Join up the synonyms (the words with similar meanings).

a

sad	large
little	excellent
big	unhappy
good	leave
go	small

b

nice	plump
nasty	pleasant
fat	giggle
call	horrible
laugh	shout

2 Copy each set of words. Underline the odd word out.
  a new   fresh   dirty   modern
  b come   garden   arrive   reach
  c home   house   building   sun
  d kick   jump   leap   bound
  e animals people   persons   folk

Unit 12 Life in ancient Egypt

Before you read the information, look at the title and the paragraph headings. How do these help you?

The River Nile

The River Nile has always been very important to Egypt. Life in Egypt depends on the water from the river. It provides water for farming.

The Pharaohs (kings of Egypt)

The kings of Egypt (the pharaohs) were very powerful. The people thought that the pharaoh was a god. He owned everything. Everyone had to do what he told them to do. The pharaohs built huge tombs. When a pharaoh died, he was buried in the tomb. The tombs were often in the shape of pyramids. When a pharaoh was buried, he was surrounded by treasure and by things to help him in the next world, such as food, clothes, furniture and weapons.

Work

In ancient Egypt, women did not go out to work. They stayed and worked at home. Many Egyptian men were farmers. Some men were builders or fishermen. Other men worked as artists. The priests and other important people did not do any farming.

Clothes

The weather in Egypt was very hot. Ancient Egyptians did not wear many clothes. Men, women and children often wore simple **robes** made of thin cloth. On their feet they wore open sandals. People, including women, shaved their heads to keep cool. They wore **wigs** for special occasions.

Children

Children in ancient Egypt grew up to do the same jobs as their parents. Girls stayed at home with their mothers. They learned to look after the home and cook. Boys worked with their fathers. They learnt to do the jobs their fathers did. They only went to school if they wanted to learn to write (to become a **scribe**).

Games

Many of the games played by ancient Egyptians are similar to games we still play today. Children played running and jumping games. They also played ball games and with wooden toys. Older children played a game like chess, called 'senet'.

1 How many paragraphs is the information divided into? *6*
2 How do the headings of each paragraph help you? *Because of the intres*
3 Why has the River Nile always been important to Egypt?
4 What happened when a pharaoh was buried? *The put all the staff.*
5 a What sort of jobs did the men do? *Buiders and fanmers*
  b What sort of jobs did the women do? *cook and tidy*
6 Do you think it was a good idea for the Egyptians to shave their heads?
  Why? *Yes so they can't get hot,*
7 Which Egyptian children went to school? *the scribes*
8 What was 'senet'? *chess game*

1 Change the verbs from the present tense to the past tense.
  a The sun <u>rises</u>. *rose*   b The sun <u>shines</u>. *shone*
  c The wind <u>blows</u>. *blue*   d The clouds <u>appear</u>. *appeared*
  e The rain <u>falls</u>. *fell*   f The earth <u>dries</u> up. *dried*
  g The sun <u>sets</u>. *set*   h The moon <u>comes</u> out. *went*

2 Now write each sentence again. Write the verbs in the future tense, like
  this:
  a The sun <u>rises</u>. *The sun will rise.*

1 Add the suffix **ful** to these nouns to change them into adjectives.
  a power – <u>powerful</u>   b use   c hope   d pain   e care
2 Change the suffix **ful** to **less** to give the opposite meaning.
  a powerful – <u>powerless</u>   b useful – *useless*
  c hopeful – *hopless*   d painful – *paintless*
  e careful – *carefuless*
3 Write the opposite of:
  a hopeless   b powerful   c careless   d painful   e useless
  hopefull   powless   careful   painless   useful
4 Write these words and add the suffixes **ful** and **less.**
  a help – <u>helpful</u> – <u>helpless</u>   b colour *colourful   coulorless*
  c thank *thankful – thankless*   d rest *restful   restless*
  e thought *thoughtful – thoughtless*

35

Unit 13 An alphabet of food

What is the poem below about? What do you notice about the way it is set out?

A is for apples that are lovely to crunch,

B is for bananas in a bunch.

C is for cake with candles alight,

D is for doughnuts so soft to bite.

E is for eggs fried in a pan,

F is for fish, catch one if you can!

G is for grapes, green and sweet,

H is for hamburger, delicious to eat.

I is for ice-cream, soft and cold,

J is for jelly in a mould.

K is for ketchup in a jar,

L is for lemon, too **sour** by far!

M is for mushrooms in a pack,

N is for nuts that are hard to crack.

O is for onions that make you cry,

P is for pancakes tossed so high.

Q is for **quiche**, made with cheese,

R is for rice, if you please.

S is for sausages, sizzling in the pan,

T is for toast covered with jam.

U is for **ugli fruit**, not a nice name,

V is for vegetables, no two the same!

W is for water melon and also for wheat,

X is for nothing I can think of to eat!

Y is for yoghurt, thick like cream,

Z is for ZZZZZZZ – all this food
makes me dream!

1 What do you notice about the way the poem is set out? *Rhyming cou...*
2 What are …
   a lovely to crunch? *apples*
   b green and sweet? *grapes*
   c hard to crack? ✓ *nuts* *mushroom* *pancakes* *sausages* *Jelly*
3 What food is given for the letter: a **M**?   b **P**?   c **S**?   d **J**?
4 No food is given for two letters. Which letters are these? Why is this? *X Z*
5 Which type of food mentioned do you like best? Why? *apple* *crunchy*
6 Which food mentioned makes you cry? *onion* *eat please some*
7 Write a word from the poem that rhymes with a sweet b cheese c name
8 Think of another food beginning with the letter: a **S**   b **P**   c **B**   d **C**

Choose the best adjective to complete each simile.
1 as __sweet__ as honey (sweet / sour)
2 as __sweet__ as a watermelon (dry / juicy) *Juicy*
3 as __flat__ as a pancake (flat / bumpy)
4 as __sour__ as a lemon (sweet / sour)
5 as __cold__ as an ice-cream (hot / cold)
6 as __light__ as a feather (light, heavy)
7 as __sharp__ as a knife (blunt / sharp)
8 as __hard__ as a rock (hard / soft)

1 Write these sets of words in alphabetical order according to their first
   letters.
   a orange, apple, melon, banana   b tea, coffee, water, milk
   c cage, ant, dance, bird   d nail, python, melon, oil
2 Write these sets of words in alphabetical order according to the second
   letter.
   a eagle, eye, egg, elephant   b deer, danger, dinner, drum
   c pigeon, parrot, peas, priest   d wood, wrist, west, winter
3 Write the following in alphabetical order:
   a the days of the week   b the months of the year

Unit 14 A good night's work

Do you think it is exciting to be a detective? Why?

The telephone rang. Detective Lee picked it up and listened. When he put it down, he turned to Detective Chang and said, 'Two people have broken into a factory. Let's go and **investigate**.'

The two detectives quickly grabbed the things they needed – **torches**, two-way radios and **handcuffs**.

They jumped into their car and raced towards the factory. As they got near, Lee turned off the lights of the car. Another empty car was parked nearby. Chang quietly called the station to check on the car. It was a stolen car.

Both men got out of the police car silently. Chang pushed open the factory door. Everything was in darkness. Lee stood and listened. He turned on his torch and shone it around. Nothing!

Chang whispered to Lee that he was going upstairs to have a look around. Lee followed him. As they crept up the stairs the two detectives heard the sound of voices. They were coming from the office where all the money was kept in the safe.

Chang took a deep breath and threw the door open. There, in the light of the torch, they saw two men. They were emptying the money from the **safe** into a sack.

'Police!' shouted Chang. 'Stay where you are. Don't move!'

The two men took no notice. They jumped to their feet and rushed towards the door. Chang was knocked over as the two men pushed past.

A man with fair hair ran towards the stairs. Lee dived and pushed the robber in the back. The robber went crashing down the stairs. Lee raced after him. In no time at all, Lee placed the handcuffs on the thief and tied him to a table. Then he went back up stairs to help Chang.

Together they searched everywhere – but could not find the second thief anywhere.

'He can't have disappeared!' Chang exclaimed. Just then they heard a **gurgling** noise. It came from a large water tank in the corner. The two detectives crept towards the tank. Lee pulled the cover off and there – almost completely covered with water, was the second thief. Lee pulled him out and led him downstairs too.

'A good night's work,' smiled Chang. The two theives did not smile. They did not agree. It was a bad night for them!

1 Name the two detectives in the story.
2 List the things the detectives took with them.
3 Why do you think Lee turned off the car lights when they got near the factory?
4 How did Lee and Chan guess someone was in the factory before they went in?
5 Where did Lee and Chan find the two men?
6 What were the two men doing when Lee and Chan first saw them?
7 Describe how Lee stopped one of the men.
8 What made Lee and Chan look in the water tank?

Copy this short story. Fill in the missing speech marks.
1 Maria said, Listen. Can you hear anything?
  Maria said, 'Listen. Can you hear anything?'
2 Peter replied, I can't hear a thing.
3 I'm sure I can hear voices! Maria insisted.
4 You're right! Someone is coming, Peter whispered.
5 Let's get out of here, Maria said.
6 Where shall we go? Peter asked.
7 Climb out of the window, Maria ordered.
8 Peter added, Don't forget to bring your torch.

1 **Divide these words into three sets according to their letter patterns.**

fair	share	chair	care	hair	bear
wear	square	tear	stair	stare	pear

2 **Choose a sensible word to complete this sentence.**
  The letters **are**, **air** and **ear** often sound the _____ .

3 **Choose the correct homophone to complete each sentence. Use a dictionary to help you if necessary.**
  a The thief said it was not _____ (fair / fare).
  b The _____ (bear / bare) lived in the woods.
  c I ate a (pair / pear).
  d I gave the robber a (stair / stare).
  e My _____ (hare / hair) got wet in the rain.

Unit 15 Famous explorers

Exploring unknown places can be very dangerous. Why do people do it?

The word 'explorer' describes someone who tries to find out more about the world. Ever since the beginning of time people have wanted to explore our world and go to places no-one has ever seen before. There have been many famous explorers over the years. Many of them were very brave. They often set out without knowing what adventures may be ahead. Here are some famous explorers from the past.

Leif Eriksson (10th century)
Leif came from Scandinavia. He travelled from Greenland across the Atlantic Ocean to Canada.

Marco Polo (13th century)
When he was 17, Marco Polo travelled to China and back. He was away from his home in Italy for 24 years. We know all about his travels because he wrote a book about them.

Ibn Battuta (14th century)
Ibn Battuta set off from his home in Arabia and travelled the world. He explored Africa, India and China.

Christopher Columbus (15th century)
Christopher Columbus was one of the most famous explorers from Europe. When he set sail in his ship, many people thought the world was flat! He sailed across the Atlantic Ocean and arrived in the West Indies.

Sir Francis Drake (16th century)
Drake set sail from England in 1577 to look for new lands. He was the first man to sail round the world.

Abel Tasman (17th century)
Abel Tasman was Dutch. He went out in search of new places to trade with. Tasman reached Australia and New Zealand.

Use the information you have read to make a chart like this:

Name of explorer (in order of date)	Century	Country that explorer came from	Place(s) visited
Leif Eriksson	10th century	Scandinavia	Greenland to Canada

Choose an adverb from the box to complete each sentence.

> bravely   quietly   smartly   patiently   slowly   soundly   carefully
> happily   suddenly   heavily

a The cat crept _quietly_ .
b The baby slept _Suddenly_ .
c The boy smiled _happily_ .
d The girl dressed _Smartly_ .
e The soldier fought _bravely_ .
f The lion waited _patiently_ .
g The car braked _Soundly_ .
h I listened _Carefully_ .
i The old man walked _Slowly_ .
j The rain fell _heavily_ .

1 Copy the words. Say each word slowly. After each word write if it has one or two syllables.
   a landed _2_
   b ship _1_
   c because _2_
   d is _1_
   e danger _2_
   f near _1_
   g swimmer _2_
   h play _1_
   i broken _2_

2 Do the word sums. Write the two-syllable words you make.
   a a + round = _around_
   b some + times = _sometime_
   c en + joy = _enjoy_
   d look + ing = _looking_
   e re + lax = _relax_
   f ex + plore = _explore_

3 Copy the words. Choose the missing double consonant to finish each.
   a su_dd_en (dd / ss)
   b be_tt_er (tt / bb)
   c le_ss_on (gg / ss)
   d no_dd_ed (dd / ll)
   e li_tt_le (tt / mm)
   f ha_pp_ens (rr / pp)
   g sma_ll_er (bb / ll)
   h ma_nn_ers (nn / mm)

4 Now write each word you made in 3 above. Split the words into two syllables.
   a sudden – sud / den

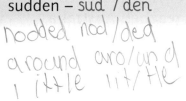
nodded nod/ded
around aro/und
little lit/tle

44

Unit 16   How to keep a bird diary

Why do people keep diaries?

A bird diary is a **record** of all the birds you have seen. Here's how you can prepare information for your bird diary:

- Find a quiet place where there are lots of birds. Birds like places where they can find food and water.
- Sit in a place where you will not disturb the birds. Don't frighten the birds with sudden movements or loud noises.
- Make notes about the birds. Look at one bird at a time. What can you see? Write about it in a small notebook. At home copy your notes up neatly into your bird diary.
- Draw pictures of the birds. Do quick drawings in your notebook. You can also take photographs of the birds. At home, copy the drawings into your bird diary. Put photographs into your bird diary, too.

It's easy to forget things. Here are some questions you should ask yourself:

- What colour is the bird? Some birds have bright colours to attract other birds. Some birds are the same colour as the land they live on, so that enemies don't see them.
- What shape are the bird's wings? Some birds have wide powerful wings. Others have small wings that move quickly when they fly. You can stick feathers in your bird diary. Remember never to touch birds' nests or steal eggs from them.
- What is the bird's beak like? Birds with short beaks, like **sparrows** and **finches**, eat seeds. Some birds, like **hoopoes**, have long sharp beaks to catch worms. **Hawks** and **eagles** have strong beaks like hooks. They eat meat.
- What are the bird's feet like? Can they grip a branch? Are they good for walking or swimming?

45

Bird: The Bald Eagle
Place: Grand Canyon
Date and Time: 5pm August 5th
Weather: warm and sunny
I saw a bald eagle. It had a white head and a white neck and tail. Its body was about 100cm long. It had enormous wings. Its beak was yellow and like a hook. Bald eagles are very rare. It was trying to catch salmon in the river. It had very large claws. I found this feather in the grass.

Janet Olearski, from *The Sunbird Mystery*
(Macmillan Education)

1 What sort of diary is being described?
2 What sort of places do birds like best?
3 Why do you think it is best to write notes in a notebook and then copy your notes up neatly when you get home?
4 Think of some difficulties there might be in making sketches of the birds.
5 Why do some birds have   a bright colours
   b the same colours as the land they live on?
6 Why do you think you should never touch birds' nests or steal their eggs?
7 List three different types of birds' beaks. Explain the differences between them.
8 How good did you think the diary entry about the bald eagle was? Why?

SENTENCE LEVEL

Copy the sentences. Cross out the word that is not needed in each sentence.
1 The bird flew over ~~above~~ the tree.
2 I couldn't see the pencil ~~not~~ anywhere.
3 The man got into ~~in~~ his car.
4 Anna and Nasrin ~~were~~ ran home.
5 The girl returned ~~it~~ the book.
6 'Come here,' Ben ~~did~~ said quietly.
7 Sam knocked at ~~on~~ the door.
8 The teacher saw ~~him~~ Alex.

WORD LEVEL

1 **Add ir to each word. Write the words you make.**
  a b_ir_d   b g_ir_l   c d_ir_t
  d f_ir_st   e b_ir_th   f st_ir_
  g ch_ir_p   h sk_ir_t   i th_ir_d
  j sh_ir_t

2 **Write the words containing:**
  a ird   b irt

3 **Write the ir word that means:**
  a something that flies bird   b the noise a bird makes chirp
  c the opposite of boy girl   d something a girl wears skirt
  e coming after second third   f being born   birth
  g to mix with a spoon stir   h coming before second first

47

Unit **17** I visited a village

There is a saying, 'If a job is worth doing, it is worth doing well.'
What do you think this means?

I visited a village
And the dancers were dancing.
They danced with all their hearts
And my whole life smiled.

I visited a school
And the teachers were teaching.
They taught with all their hearts
And my whole life smiled.

I visited a clinic
And the nurses were nursing.
They nursed with all their hearts
And my whole life smiled.

I visited a farm
And the farmers were farming.
They farmed with all their hearts
And my whole life smiled.

I came back home
And my parents were waving.
They waved with all their hearts
And my whole life smiled.

Moses Kaliwo, from *On the Poetry Bus*
(Macmillan Education)

1 What is the title of the poem?
2 Who wrote the poem?
3 How many verses are there?
4 How many lines are there in each verse?
5 Is it a rhyming poem? Do you think this matters?
6 List the places the poet visited in order.
7 What do you notice about the last line of each verse?
8 Here is an old African saying. 'If you want to be happy, you must have something to do, something or someone to love and something to hope for.' Say what you think it means.

SENTENCE LEVEL

Choose the best preposition to complete each sentence.
1 I hid _behind_ the tree. (behind / above)
2 The boy jumped _____ the river. (off / into)
3 The girl fell _____ her bicycle. (through / off)
4 The man swam _____ the shore. (towards / down)
5 The bus stopped _____ the shop. (over / near)
6 The children walked _____ the tunnel. (between / through)
7 The baby fell _____ the stairs. (up / down)
8 I stood _____ my mum and dad. (between / above)

WORD LEVEL

village place stage cage lace face trace rage space page

1 **Copy the words and write them in two sets – ace words and age words.**
2 **Choose ace or age to complete each of these words:**
   a vill _age_   b l _____   c st _____
   d f_____   e c _____   f tr _____
   g sp_____   h pl _____   i r _____
   j p _____
3 **Copy these words. Underline ace or age in each.**
   a palace   b postage   c surface
   d cottage   e bandage   f engage
   g fireplace   h graceful   i braces

Martha's mistakes

Do you ever have days when nothing seems to go right? Read about Martha. She often does!

Martha wanted to help, but that was not easy for Martha. Whenever she helped, things went wrong. She tried and tried, but it was no good. When she washed the clothes, she dropped them in the dirt. When she went to the market, she forgot her money. When she **mended** Mother's chair, it broke again. When she looked after the baby, he fell down.

Martha was not happy about all this. When the other children helped, everything was right. When she helped, everything was wrong. She always made mistakes.

Martha did not know why she made mistakes. The other children never dropped things or forgot things or broke things, so why did she?

If the other children played football, they never fell in the dirt. Martha always fell over and got dirty.

If they wrote in their books, their pencils never broke. Martha's pencil always broke.

If they climbed trees, they never hurt themselves. Martha always hurt herself.

If they looked for their bags or their shoes or their crayons or their pullovers, they always found them. Martha could never find anything.

They were usually early for school. Martha was usually late.

They remembered their homework. Martha forgot hers.

Mistakes always happened and things went wrong.

But although Martha made mistakes, everybody liked her. She was never angry or nasty or rude. She was funny and kind and polite, and she had lots of friends.

One morning when Martha wanted to help, her mother said, 'No thank you, Martha. Not now, because it's time for school.' But then Martha's mother stopped and thought again. She was very busy. She wanted to clean the house. She wanted to make a new dress. She wanted to iron some clothes. Perhaps Martha could help.

Mother had a bag of sugar for Auntie. Could Martha take the sugar to her?

She had some salt for Grandmother. Could Martha take the salt to her?

She had a pot of jam for Grandfather. Could Martha take the jam to him?

She had some paint for Uncle. Could Martha take the paint to him?

Martha's mother thought hard and then said, 'Wait a minute, Martha. Perhaps you can help me.'

Martha was very happy.

'Good,' she said. 'What can I do?'

Lorna Evans, *Martha's Mistakes* (Macmillan Education)

1 What was Martha's main problem? *mistakes*
2 List three things that went wrong when Martha tried to help. *fell. hurt. dirty*
3 Why did everybody like Martha? *funny kind polite*
4 Do you feel sorry for Martha? Give a reason for your answer. *Yes she did her best*
5 Why did Martha's mother ask Martha to help? *She had a lot of things to do*
6 What jobs did she ask Martha to do? *Clean, tidy and filing*
7 How do you think Martha felt when her mother asked her to help? *amazed*
8 What do you think will happen? *She won't drop a single thing after that*

Punctuate these sentences correctly.
1 what time is it martha asked
   'What time is it?' Martha asked.
2 what a lovely view the king exclaimed *"what a lovely view" the king ex*
3 where did I put my glasses the boy asked *Where did I put my glasses?*
4 martha sam ben and tom are running to school *Martha, Sam, ben and tom*
5 the footballer fell over and broke his leg *The footballer, fell over and hurt*
6 the frightened child ran away to london *the frightened child, to lond*
7 the boy who was talking was told off by the teacher *The boy who was*
8 it's a lovely day mr jones said *"It a lovely day" mr Jones said*

1 **Copy these words. Complete each word with ur.**
   a h*ur*t   b b*ur*n
   c t*ur*n   d f*ur*
   e c*ur*l   f p*ur*se
   g n*ur*se   h c*ur*ve
   i s*ur*name   j Th*ur*sday

2 **Choose the correct ur word to complete each sentence.**
   a Martha fell over and *hurt* her arm. (curl / hurt)
   b A wheel can *turn*. (burn / turn)
   c A fire can *burn*. (burn / turn)
   d You put money in a *purse*. (purse / fur)
   e *Thursday* comes after Wednesday. (Saturday / Thursday)
   f A cat has soft *fur*. (curve / fur)

53

Unit 19 Anansi and the alligator eggs

Anansi is a spider who is very clever. He is always tricking others.
How do you think he tricks the alligator?

Characters: Anansi, Mr Alligator, Mrs Alligator, Deaf Fish, Mute Fish

Storyteller:	This is the story of Anansi, who met Mr Alligator by the river on his way home.
Annasi:	How nice to see you, Mr Alligator. I have some cherries for you.
Mr Alligator:	Thank you. My wife loves cherries. Do come to dinner with us.
Storyteller:	Anansi was worried about going with Mr Alligator in case he ate him, but Mr Alligator insisted. They ate and ate until very late.
Anansi:	Thank you for the lovely dinner, but I must be on my way now.

Mrs Alligator:	Oh no, my dear. It is far too late. You must sleep with the children.
Anansi;	All right, Mrs Alligator. If you insist.
Mrs Alligator:	I do, I do!
Storyteller:	The ten children were still alligator eggs in the muddy **river bank** next to the house. Anansi soon fell asleep, but in the night he woke up feeling rather hungry.
Anansi:	I'll just eat one of these eggs. Nobody will notice.
Storyteller:	The egg was so delicious, that Anansi could not stop and he ate another egg, and another until only one egg was left!
Anansi:	Oh dear! What will I do? I've eaten nine of the eggs and there's only one left. Mr Alligator will eat me up if I don't leave right now. I'll go before Mr Alligator gets up.
Storyteller:	But just as Anansi was about to leave, Mr Alligator appeared.
Mr Alligator:	Good morning, Anansi. You're up bright and early.
Anansi:	Yes, I was just leaving. I didn't want to disturb you.
Mr Alligator:	Please help me wash the eggs first.
Storyteller:	Anansi was just wondering what he could do, when he had an idea.
Anansi:	All right, but I will do it for you. Sit down and relax.
Storyteller:	Anansi washed the one egg carefully and took it to Mr Alligator.
Anansi:	Isn't it a beautiful egg? Is that clean enough, Mr Alligator? I polished it especially on my handkerchief.
Mr Alligator:	You have done a very good job.
Anansi:	I'll put it back and get another one.
Storyteller:	Anansi took the egg back to the nest, put mud on it and took it to Mr Alligator.
Mr Alligator:	Just wipe off the mud and that egg will be fine.
Anansi:	Silly Mr Alligator. He doesn't realise it's the same egg!
Storyteller:	Anansi did the same thing to the rest of the eggs. Mr Alligator thought Anansi had cleaned ten eggs.
Mr Alligator:	Thank you for cleaning all ten eggs. I'll ask my friends the fish to take you home. One doesn't speak and the other doesn't hear, but they are very kind.
Anansi:	Thank you very much.

Storyteller:	Anansi told the fish to go quickly, and they began to row him to the other side of the river. Meanwhile Mr Alligator discovered he had been tricked.
Mr Alligator:	Come back! Come back, Anansi, you **rascal**!
Deaf Fish:	What's he saying? I can't hear a thing. Why is Mr Alligator jumping up and down?
Anansi:	It's nothing. He's just waving goodbye.
Mute Fish:	Gulp! Gulp!
Deaf Fish:	What? What? What are you trying to say?
Anansi:	He says there will be a storm. Row faster!
Storyteller:	The fish kept rowing until they reached the other side – and that is how Anansi escaped from Mr Alligator.

1 Name the characters in the play. *Annansi Mr Alligator Mrsaliggate Deaf*
2 a Why did Anansi stay the night? b What happened during the night? *Mute*
3 How did Anansi feel *Story teller*
   a when he was invited to dinner? *after doing the problem*
   b in the morning when Mr Alligator saw him? *She was so Proud*
   c when he escaped in the boat? *Mr alligator was really angry*
4 What problems did the two fish have? *one was Deaf and Mute*
5 What sort of character did Ananasi have? Explain your answer. *Spider*
6 Were you sorry for Mr Alligator? Give a reason. *yes why*
7 What do you think Mr Alligator would have done if he had caught Anansi? *Punsh*
8 In the play, how does each character know when to speak? *their name*

Copy and complete this chart.

Past tense	Present tense	Future tense
Yesterday Anansi washed.	Today Anansi is washing.	Tomorrow Anansi will wash.
Yesterday Anansi played.	Today Anansi is playing.	*Today Anansi will Play*
Yesterday Thandi saw Anansi. *Hand on the other one*	*Today ananis is ?*	
	Today Anansi is cleaning.	Tomorrow Anansi will crawl.
Yesterday Anansi swept.	*Today for the*	*the woman*
will will hary	Today Anansi is working.	Tomorrow Anansi will run.

1 **Choose er or or to complete each of these words.**
   a alligat*or*   b spid*er*
   c g*or*rilla   d h*or*se
   e panth*er*   f p*er*fect
   g st*or*k   h butt*er*fly

2 **Now write the words from 1 in alphabetical order.**

Unit 20 Endangered animals

Some animals in the world are in danger of dying out. Can you name any?

The problem

Some species of animals are rare. If their numbers get too small, there will not be enough adults left to breed. These animals could become extinct. We call animals like this an *endangered species*.

A species of animal needs two things so that they can continue to live.

- adults that can have babies.
- somewhere to live, where food can be found.

Humans are the main danger to many animals.

- People hunt animals to sell.
- People hunt animals for sport.
- People kill animals until there are none left.

Lemurs are an endangered species

People destroy the places where animals live.

- People cut down forests for **timber** and to make farmland.
- People build towns where there used to be fields.
- People **pollute** the soil, air, seas and rivers.

Forest being cut down and burnt to make way for farmland.

Saving endangered animals

Some zoos try to get their rare animals to **breed**. When the babies become adults, they can be taken to live in the wild. In this way, some animals have been saved from becoming extinct. But even the best zoos cannot make the zoo home exactly like the animals' real home. The weather and food might be different. In the zoo, animals are not hunted. But when zoo animals are taken to live in their natural homes, they have to learn how to look after themselves.

The best way to help an endangered species is to start a breeding centre in the animals' own country. As well as saving the animals, their natural home has to be saved too. Some countries have Game Reserves or National Parks where wildlife cannot be hunted or killed. The land cannot be farmed or built on.

Spotlight on Orang-utans

Orang-utans are an endangered species. There are probably fewer than 10,000 living in the wild. Orang-utans are only found in the forests of Borneo, Indonesia and Sumatra. Orang-utans are plant eaters. They have no natural enemies, apart from humans. They are very intelligent. Orang-utans live alone or in small family groups. A young orang-utan stays with its mother until it is about ten years old. Then it is able to look after itself in the forest.

Fascinating Facts about Orang-utans

- 'Orang-utan' means 'wild man of the forests.'
- Orang-utans hate rain. During a rain storm they might make an umbrella out of a leafy branch.
- Orang-utans spend most of their lives in trees. At night they make a nest of leaves and branches to sleep in.
- Orang-utans eat fruit, nuts and leaves. Sometimes they eat birds' eggs and insects.

Spotlight on the Sepilok Orang-utan Centre

Sepilok is in Borneo. It is a place where people can see orang-utans in their natural home, the **rainforest**. The Centre teaches the young orang-utans to live in the forest. Sepilok has saved many orang-utans from being killed. Some have been released to live in the forest. Some have bred with wild orang-utans and had babies.

In 1957 Sepilok was made into a Game Reserve. Now no more trees can be cut down. Since 1963 Sepilok has rescued many young orang-utans. Some orang-utans lost their mothers when their forests were cut down. Others were rescued from people who stole them from the wild to sell as pets.

A feeding platform at Sepilok

Endangered Species, adapted from Living Earth Level 2 (Macmillan)

1 What does 'endangered species' mean?
2 List the reasons given why humans are a danger to other species of animals.
3 Say what you think the word 'extinct' means.
4 How do Game Reserves and National Parks help protect some animals?
5 List three things you found interesting about orang-utans.
6 Describe some of the important work done at Sepilok.
7 Do you know the names of any other endangered species of animals?
8 Does it matter if some species of animals die out? Say what you think.

1 Match up each singular noun with its plural.

deer	sheep
tooth	deer
sheep	fish
fish	geese
foot	men
man	feet
child	teeth
goose	children

2 Which nouns are the same in the singular and plural?

3 Work out what these are:
a a pair of tr_ _sers   b a pair of sci_ _ors   c a pair of gla_ _es

1 Copy the words. Add the prefix **en** to each word. Match the best definition to each word.

a ___danger – _endanger_   to force something
b ___able – _____   to make rich
c ___force – _____   to put into danger
d ___rich – _____   to put a circle round something
e ___circle – _____   to make it possible

2 Copy the words. Add the prefix **re** to each word.
a _re_ turn   b ___pay   c ___new   d ___fill   e ___consider

3 Now write the meaning of each **re** word in 2 above.
Do it like this: a return means 'to come back again'.

Glossary of Language Terms

Adjective An **adjective** is a describing word. It gives more meaning to a noun. a **fierce** lion
To compare nouns we use **comparative** or **superlative** adjectives. fat – **fatter** – **fattest**

Adverb An **adverb** gives more meaning to a verb. It often ends in **ly**. The girl ran **quickly**.

Alphabetical order When we put words in order according to the letter or letters they begin with, we say they are in **alphabetical order**.
For example: apple, bug, cat, desk

Author An **author** is someone who writes books.

Characters **Characters** are the names of people, animals or things that appear in stories.

Comma A **comma** is a punctuation mark. It tells you to pause.
I ate an apple**,** an orange and a banana.

Conjunction A **conjunction** is a joining word. Conjunctions are often used to join two sentences together.
I went home **and** I watched television.

Consonant Our alphabet is divided up into vowels and **consonants**. The vowels are **a**, **e**, **i**, **o** and **u**. All the other letters are consonants.

Contraction A **contraction** is when two words are made into one word, by leaving some letters out. don't = do not

Exclamation An **exclamation** is a sentence which shows that we feel strongly about something. It always ends with an **exclamation mark**.
Come back at once**!**

Full stop A **full stop** is a dot showing that a sentence has ended.

Homophone **Homophones** are words that sound the same but have a different meaning.
I have a **pain** in my stomach.
I broke the **pane** of glass.

Instruction An **instruction** is when we tell people to do something, or teach them how to do something.

Letter A **letter pattern** is a group of letters which occur often in words.

Pattern Remembering letter patterns helps us with spelling. p**ark**, b**ark**, m**ark**

Noun A **noun** is a naming word. It can be the name of a person, place or thing.
a boy, a river, a pencil, an ox
A **collective noun** is the name of a group of something. For example: a flock of sheep.

Opposite **Opposites** are words whose meanings are as different as possible from each other.
big   small

Paragraph A **paragraph** is a group of sentences that deals with one main idea or topic.

Plural **Plural** means more than one. (See also **Singular**.) one snake but two **snakes**

Poem A **poem** is a piece of writing that is imaginative. It is written in lines. The lines may or may not rhyme.

Poet A **poet** is someone who writes poems.

Prefix A **prefix** is a group of letters we add to the beginning of a word to change its meaning.
happy   **un**happy

Pronoun We use a **pronoun** in place of a noun. When the girl walked in the rain, **she** got wet. (she = the girl)

Punctuation **Punctuation** helps us make sense of what we read. Punctuation marks make writing easier for us to understand. These are all punctuation marks:
Full stops .   Commas ,   Question marks ?
Exclamation marks !   Speech marks ' '

Question We ask a **question** when we want to find something out. A question always ends with a question mark. May I have an apple**?**

Rhyme A **rhyme** occurs when two words have an ending that sound the same.
The **frog** sat on the **log**.

Simile A **simile** is when we compare one thing with another. For example: The child's skin was as smooth as silk.

Singular **Singu**lar means 'one'. a **snake**, an **apple** (See also **Plural**.)

Speech marks When we write down what someone says, we put it inside **speech marks**.
The lady said, '**I'm hungry.**'

Suffix A **suffix** is a group of letters we add to the end of a word, to change its meaning.
spider   spider**s**   cook   cook**ing**

Syllable Longer words may be broken into smaller parts, called **syllables**.
cat has one syllable
catching has two syllables (cat + ching)

Synonym **Synonyms** are words with the same, or similar, meanings. **sad** = **unhappy**

Title A **title** is the name we give a book or something we have made or written.

Verb A **verb** is a 'being' or 'doing' word.
The lion **was** huge. It **roared** loudly.

Verb tenses **Verbs** may be written in different **tenses**. The tense of a verb changes according to the time of the action. For example:
Now I **am riding** a bicycle. (**present tense**)
Yesterday I **rode** a bicycle. (**past tense**)
Tomorrow I **will ride** a bicycle. (**future tense**)

Verse A poem is often divided into parts (**verses**).

Vowels There are five **vowels** in the alphabet – **a, e, i, o** and **u**. Most words contain at least one vowel. (See also **Consonants**.)